12 Piazzolla Tangos for Easy Piano

Arranged by Rachel Chapin

ISBN 978-1-4950-5762-5

DISTRIBUTED BY

7777 W. BLUEMOUND RD. P.O. BOX 13819 MILWAUKEE, WI 53213

For all works contained herein:
Unauthorized copying, arranging, adapting, recording, Internet posting, public performance,
or other distribution of the printed music in this publication is an infringement of copyright.
Infringers are liable under the law.

www.boosey.com
www.halleonard.com

Astor Piazzolla
(1921–1992)

Astor Piazzolla was the foremost composer and ambassador of tango music, who carried the signature sound of Argentina to clubs and concert halls around the world. By blending tango with elements of classical music and jazz, Piazzolla sometimes drew fire from tango traditionalists in his native country, even as he won a broad new audience for his bold, uncompromising style.

From the beginning, Piazzolla's music was strongly influenced by his experiences living and studying abroad. He was born in 1921 in Mar del Plata, on the coast south of Buenos Aires, but lived in New York City from 1924 to 1937. In New York the young Piazzolla tuned into the vibrant jazz scene and leading composers, arrangers, and bandleaders such as Duke Ellington and Cab Calloway. At age 12, Piazzolla received his first bandoneon, a large and complex type of button accordion that is the principal voice of tango, and began playing music from the classical repertoire. Soon after his family returned to Argentina in 1937, Piazzolla joined the popular tango orchestra of Anibal Troilo and—while still a teenager—established himself as a talented bandoneon player and arranger.

In Argentina, Piazzolla continued to study classical music, too, with the composer Alberto Ginastera and others. In 1954, Piazzolla's composition "Buenos Aires" (for symphony orchestra with bandoneon) won him a scholarship to study in Paris with influential teacher Nadia Boulanger, who was mentor to Aaron Copland, Virgil Thomson, and many other composers. At the time, Piazzolla was composing in the European classical style, yet Boulanger encouraged him to find his own voice by tapping into his passion for tango. Back in Argentina in the late 1950s, Piazzolla did just that, laying the groundwork for what became known as tango nuevo—new tango.

In 1960 he formed his seminal group Quinteto Tango Nuevo, featuring bandoneon alongside violin, guitar, piano, and bass in an ensemble style intended for the concert stage rather than dance hall, tango's traditional venue. In the ensuing years Piazzolla's music increasingly used dissonance, metrical shifts, counterpoint, and other techniques inspired by modern classical composition and jazz orchestras. In Argentina, where tango is a source of national pride and identity, some tango purists were incensed by these radical departures from tradition, and in the late 1960s even Argentina's military government criticized Piazzolla for being too avant-garde. Audiences in the United States and Europe, however, responded enthusiastically to Piazzolla's innovations, and eventually the controversies in Argentina faded as Piazzolla's artistic accomplishments became clear.

Piazzolla relocated to Europe in the mid-1970s and performed worldwide for the next decade while composing a wide range of music, from concertos to film and theater scores. He returned to Buenos Aires in 1985, where he remained until his death in 1992, at the age of 71.

Piazzolla left behind a huge body of music—more than 750 works—and classic recordings such as *Adiós Nonino* and *Tango: Zero Hour*, as well as collaborations with artists as diverse as poet/author Jorge Luis Borges (*El Tango*), jazz vibraphonist Gary Burton (*The New Tango*), and the Kronos Quartet (*Five Tango Sensations*). In 1986, Piazzolla's music was featured in the Broadway hit *Tango Argentino*. In the years since Piazzolla's death, a broad range of artists have continued to interpret and record his music, from guitarist David Tanenbaum (*El Porteño*) to cellist Yo-Yo Ma (*Soul of the Tango*). In 2001 Amadeus Press published *Astor Piazzolla: A Memoir*, the remarkable life story (as told to journalist Natalio Gorin) of one of the 20th century's true musical iconoclasts.

CHANSON DE LA NAISSANCE

(Song of the Birth)

from *Famille d'artistes*

By ASTOR PIAZZOLLA

© Copyright by Lime Green Music Ltd.
This arrangement © 2016 by Lime Green Music Ltd.
Copyright for All Countries. All Rights Reserved.

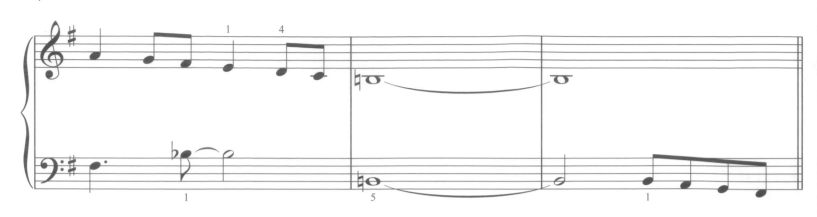

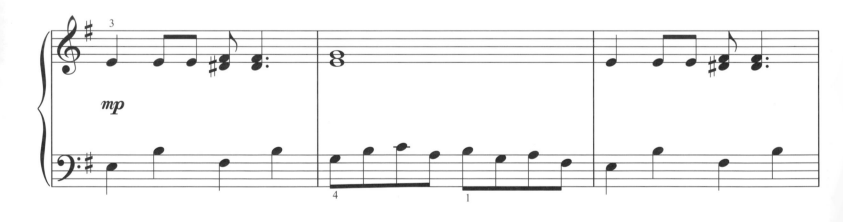

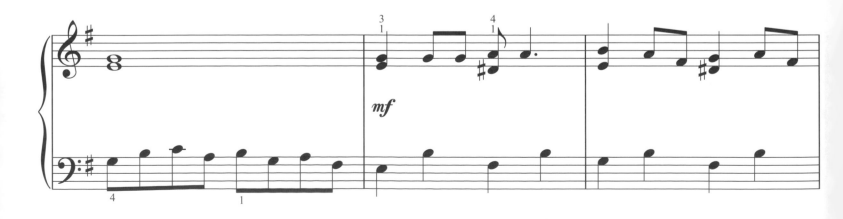

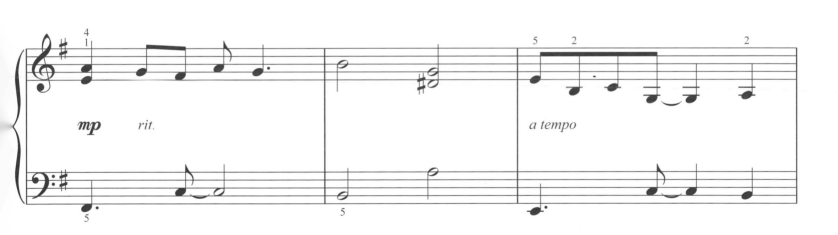

AUSENCIAS
(The Absent)

By ASTOR PIAZZOLLA

Tempo molto rubato

© Copyright by Lime Green Music Ltd.
This arrangement © 2016 by Lime Green Music Ltd.
Copyright for All Countries. All Rights Reserved.

To Coda ⊕ **A tempo (non rubato)**

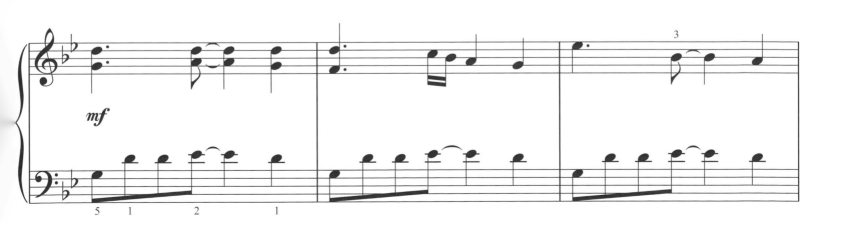

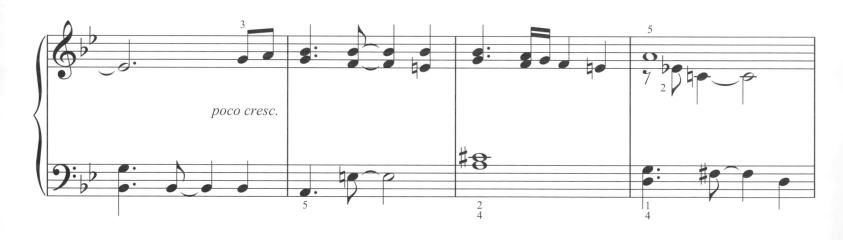

Meno mosso

D.S. al Coda

CODA

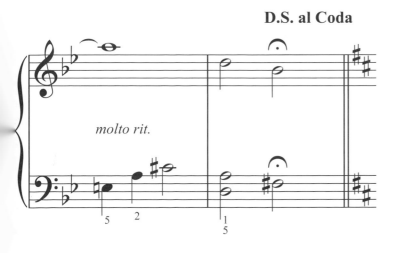

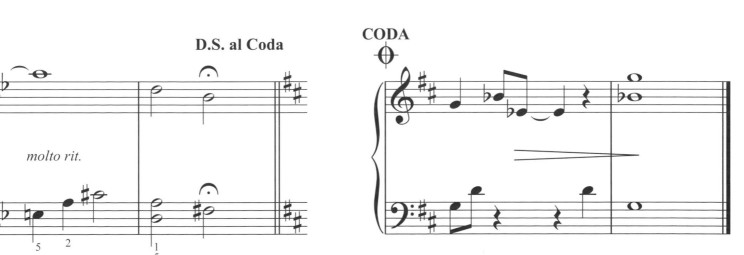

molto rit.

EL VIAJE
(The Voyage)

By ASTOR PIAZZOLLA

Andante malinconico

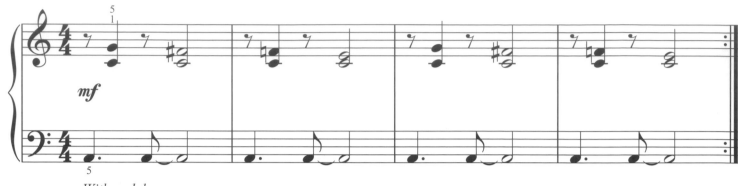

With pedal

© Copyright by Lime Green Music Ltd.
This arrangement © 2016 by Lime Green Music Ltd.
Copyright for All Countries. All Rights Reserved.

dim. al fine

MILONGA FOR THREE

By ASTOR PIAZZOLLA

© Copyright by Lime Green Music Ltd.
This arrangement © 2016 by Lime Green Music Ltd.
Copyright for All Countries. All Rights Reserved.

Slightly faster

Slightly faster again

LIBERTANGO

By ASTOR PIAZZOLLA

Copyright © 1974 Curci Edizioni S.r.l. and A. Pagani Ediz Mus S.r.l.
Copyright Renewed
This arrangement Copyright © 2016 Curci Edizioni S.r.l. and A. Pagani Ediz Mus S.r.l.
All Rights Reserved   Used by Permission

LOS SUEÑOS
(Dreams)
from *Sur*

By ASTOR PIAZZOLLA

Moderately

© Copyright by Lime Green Music Ltd.
This arrangement © 2016 by Lime Green Music Ltd.
Copyright for All Countries. All Rights Reserved.

Meno mosso

A tempo

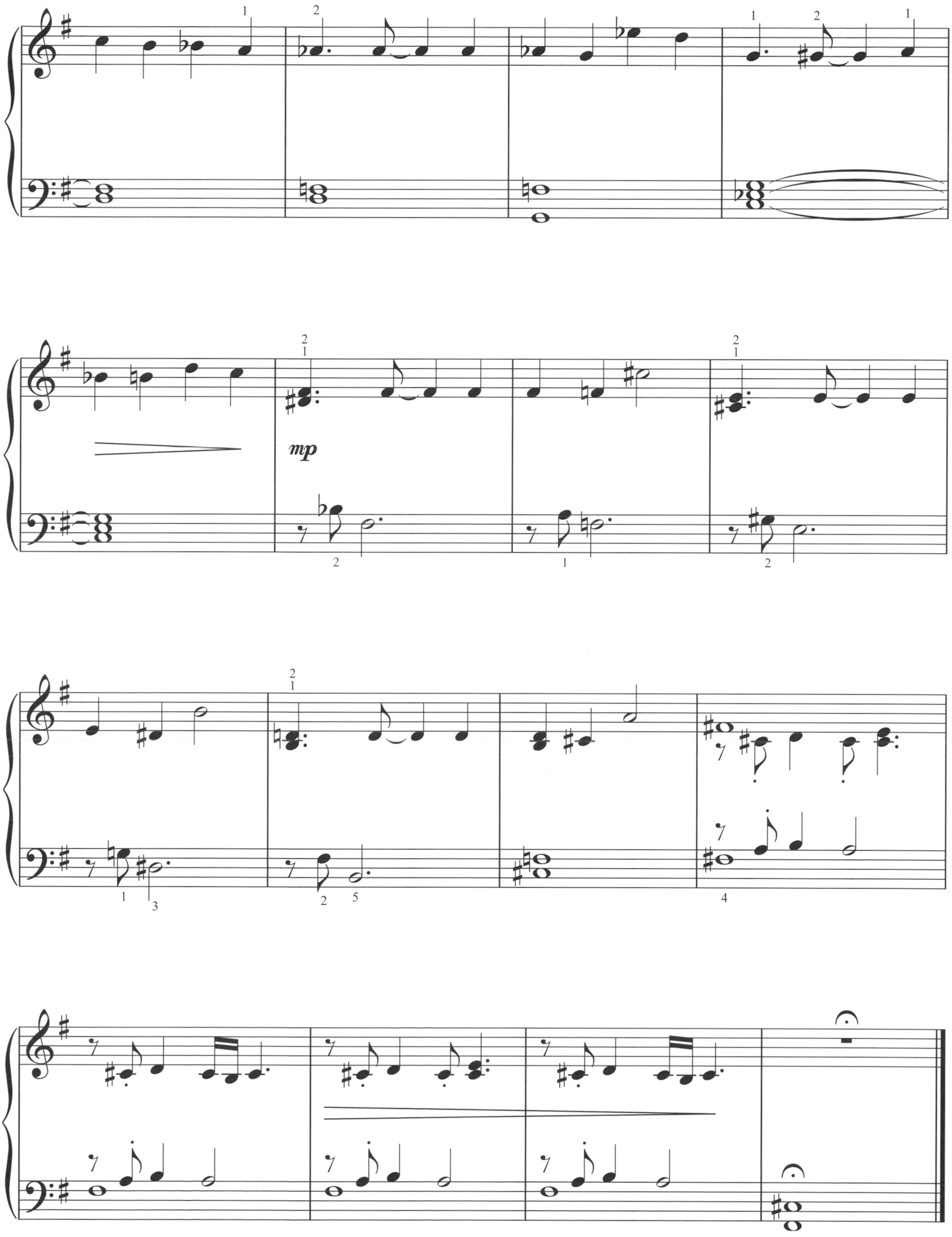
mp

OBLIVION

By ASTOR PIAZZOLLA

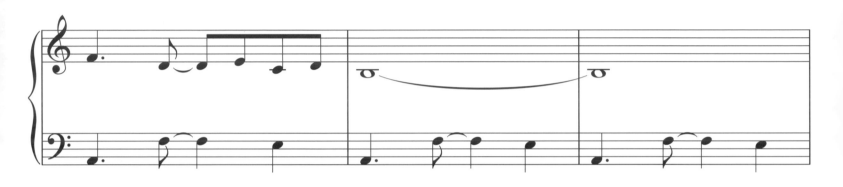

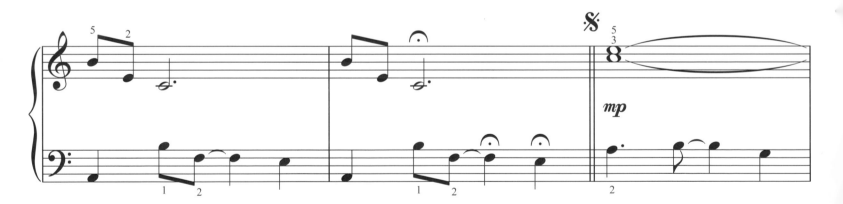

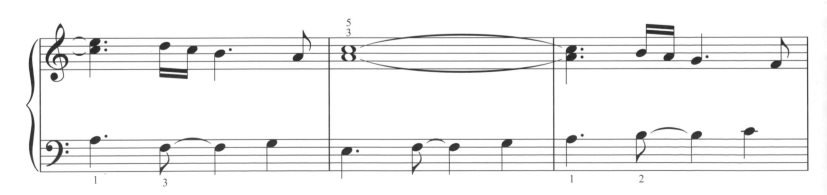

© 1984 by A. PAGANI S.r.l. Edizioni Musicali, Fino Mornasco (CO) Italy
This arrangement © 2016 by A. PAGANI S.r.l. Edizioni Musicali, Fino Mornasco (CO) Italy
Rights for USA Controlled by Stella Solaris Music
All Rights Reserved   Used by Permission

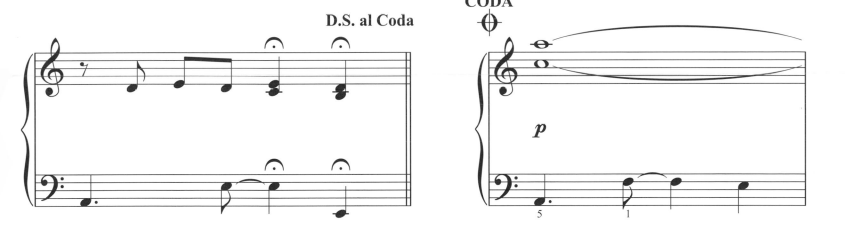

SENSUEL
(Sensual)
from *A Midsummer Night's Dream*

By ASTOR PIAZZOLLA

© Copyright by Lime Green Music Ltd.
This arrangement © 2016 by Lime Green Music Ltd.
Copyright for All Countries. All Rights Reserved.

SENTIMENTAL

from *Famille d'artistes*

By ASTOR PIAZZOLLA

© Copyright by Lime Green Music Ltd.
This arrangement © 2016 by Lime Green Music Ltd.
Copyright for All Countries. All Rights Reserved.

SIN RUMBO
(Aimless)

By ASTOR PIAZZOLLA

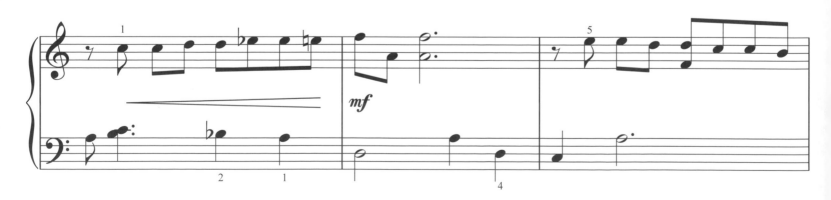

© Copyright by Lime Green Music Ltd.
This arrangement © 2016 by Lime Green Music Ltd.
Copyright for All Countries. All Rights Reserved.

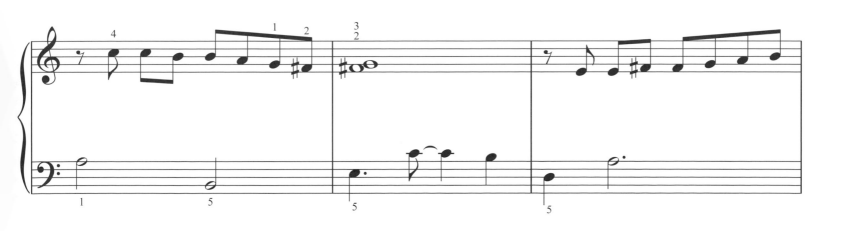

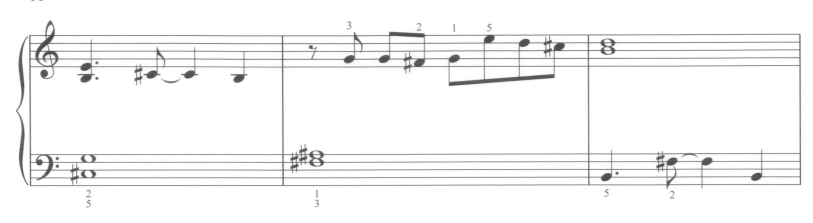

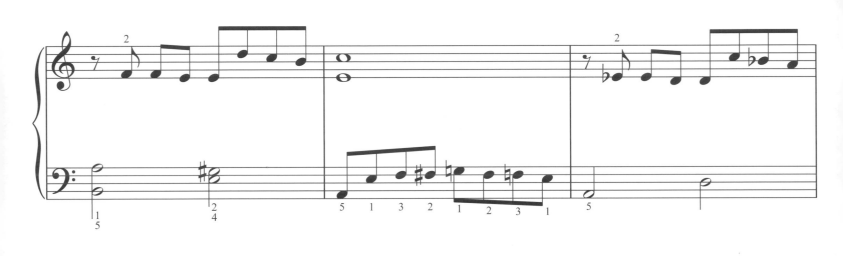

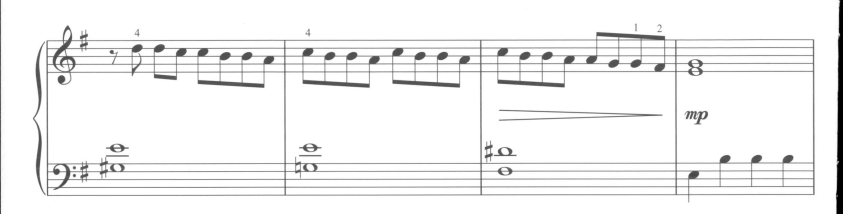

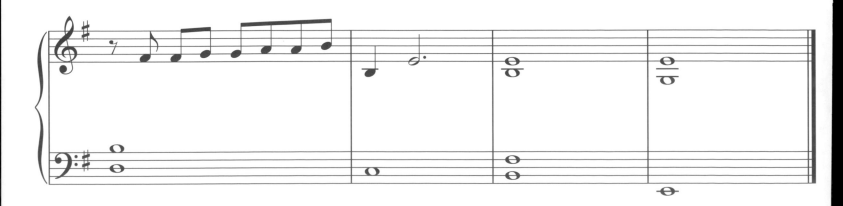

VUELVO AL SUR
(I'm Returning South)

By ASTOR PIAZZOLLA

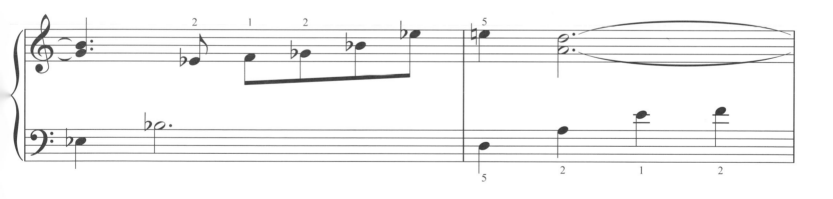

© Copyright by Lime Green Music Ltd.
This arrangement © 2016 by Lime Green Music Ltd.
Copyright for All Countries. All Rights Reserved.

Moderately

STREET TANGO

By ASTOR PIAZZOLLA

© Copyright by Lime Green Music Ltd.
This arrangement © 2016 by Lime Green Music Ltd.
Copyright for All Countries. All Rights Reserved.

Molto meno mosso

mp

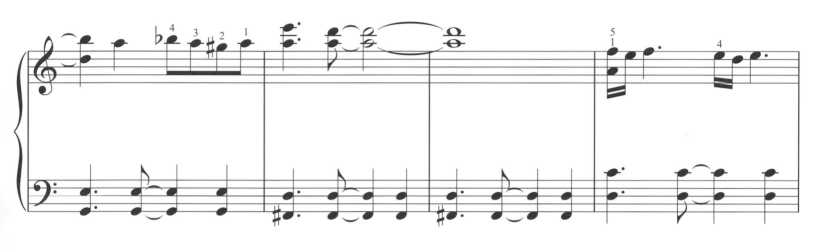

Piu mosso